INTERNET
PASSWORD
LOGBOOK

Quarto.com

© 2026 Quarto Publishing Group USA Inc.

First Published in 2026 by Cool Springs Press, an imprint of The Quarto Group,
100 Cummings Center, Suite 265-D, Beverly, MA 01915, USA.
T (978) 282-9590 F (978) 283-2742

Cool Springs Press titles are also available at discount for retail, wholesale,
promotional, and bulk purchase. For details, contact the Special Sales Manager by
email at specialsales@quarto.com or by mail at The Quarto Group, Attn: Special
Sales Manager, 100 Cummings Center, Suite 265-D, Beverly, MA 01915, USA.

30 29 28 27 26   1 2 3 4 5

ISBN: 978-1-57715-618-5

Design and Page Layout: Samantha J. Bednarek, samanthabednarek.com
Horticultural Reviewer: Botanist Scott Zona

Printed in Malaysia

Illustration on previous page: Symphyotrichum, Mary Emily Eaton, 1916
Illustration on opposite page: Coreopsis, Mary Emily Eaton, 1916

AMERICAN HORTICULTURAL SOCIETY

INTERNET
PASSWORD
LOGBOOK

COOL
SPRINGS
PRESS

Magnolia, Pierre Joseph Redouté, 1801

MEET THE AMERICAN HORTICULTURAL SOCIETY

Founded in 1922, the nonprofit American Horticultural Society (AHS) is one of the most respected and longstanding member-based national gardening organizations in North America. The society's membership includes more than 22,000 aspiring, new, and experienced gardeners, plant enthusiasts, and horticultural professionals, as well as numerous regional and national partner organizations. Through its educational programs, awards, and publications, the AHS inspires a culture of gardening and horticultural practices that creates and sustains healthy, beautiful communities and a livable planet. AHS is headquartered at River Farm, a 27-acre (1 ha) site overlooking the Potomac River that is part of George Washington's original farmlands in Alexandria, Virginia. The AHS website is www.ahsgardening.org.

ABOUT THE ILLUSTRATIONS

The collected botanical illustrations in this book were created between the years 1774 and 1925 by their noted illustrators. The AHS would like to thank the Smithsonian Institution, the New York Botanical Garden, the Biodiversity Heritage Library, and the New York Public Library Digital Collections for their use. The book's cover features an illustration from Edith S. Clements published in 1920. The endpaper illustrations were drawn by Edith S. Clements in 1920.

TIPS FOR MAKING
STRONG PASSWORDS

This password logbook provides a handy and organized way to track usernames, passwords, and log-in information for 400 different websites and six devices. However, it's up to you to create strong passwords from the start. Here are some tips for crafting secure passwords that hackers are less likely to crack.

- **Create long passwords.** A minimum of 8 characters is recommended for passwords; however, longer is always better. Aim for the maximum number of characters each website permits.

- **Combine characters.** Use a combination of letters (both upper- and lowercase), numbers, and symbols. Do not use all letters or all numbers.

- **Be random.** Rather than relying on a real word or a number already associated with you (such as a birthday or anniversary date, license plate, phone number, or even a nickname), select random combinations of letters, numbers, and symbols. Never use real words or number combinations already associated with you.

- **Avoid personal connections.** Never use the names of your partner, children, grandchildren, pets, streets, towns, etc., in passwords. All of these present a security vulnerability.

- **Nonsense is best.** The best passwords are not words at all, but rather nonsensical combinations of characters. Avoid foreign words and phrases too.

- **Skip the strings.** Don't use numbers or characters in string—or reverse string—order (for example, XYZ or 54321).

- **A unique password for every site.** Never reuse passwords from one website to the next. Each site should have its own unique password.

- **Change is good.** Changing passwords on a regular basis is essential for internet security. Now that you have this book, there's no need to worry about remembering new passwords when you change them. Each website entry in this book has space to log three password changes.

TIPS FOR KEEPING
PASSWORDS SAFE

1. Do not log into websites using your personal usernames or passwords while on public computers or while on public Wi-Fi. This includes sites like the library, a coffee shop, the mall, a restaurant, public transit, or the airport.

2. Do not share your usernames or passwords with other people. Keep them private and certainly don't text or email them to anyone.

3. Do not put any information on social media a hacker could use to decipher a password. If you've created strong passwords using the tips in the previous section, this is a non-issue as you will not be using birthdays, pet or family names, or the like.

4. Change your passwords often and use a different one for each website (it's worth repeating!).

5. Keep this password logbook in a safe place; do not travel with it or take it to public places. Remove the paper band around the front cover so "Internet Password Logbook" is not announced on the cover. Put this book in a private and secure location.

Note: *The publisher of this book cannot be held responsible or liable for any damages, errors, consequences, or losses that may result from any user recording and storing private data in this book. The publisher is also not responsible for any damages, errors, consequences, or losses that may result, despite following the tips in this book.*

Papaver, Nicolas-François Regnault, 1774

Computer/Phone/Tablet 1

Username _____

Password _____

_____

_____

Recovery key _____

Computer/Phone/Tablet 2

Username _____

Password _____

_____

_____

Recovery key _____

Computer/Phone/Tablet 3

Username _____

Password _____

_____

_____

Recovery key _____

Computer/Phone/Tablet 4

Username _____

Password _____

_____

_____

Recovery key _____

Computer/Phone/Tablet 5

Username _____

Password _____

_____

_____

Recovery key _____

Computer/Phone/Tablet 6

Username _____

Password _____

_____

_____

Recovery key _____

Name/Company _____

Username _____

Password _____

Notes _____

_____

_____

Name/Company _____

Username _____

Password _____

Notes _____

_____

_____

Name/Company _____

Username _____

Password _____

Notes _____

_____

_____

Name/Company _____

Username _____

Password _____

Notes _____

_____

_____

Name/Company _____

Username _____

Password _____

Notes _____

_____

_____

Name/Company _____

Username _____

Password _____

Notes _____

_____

_____

Name/Company _____

Username _____

Password _____

Notes _____

_____

_____

Name/Company _____

Username _____

Password _____

Notes _____

_____

_____

Name/Company _____

Username _____

Password _____

Notes _____

_____

_____

Name/Company _____

Username _____

Password _____

Notes _____

_____

_____

Name/Company _____

Username _____

Password _____

Notes _____

_____

_____

Name/Company _____

Username _____

Password _____

Notes _____

_____

_____

Name/Company _____

Username _____

Password _____

Notes _____

_____

_____

Name/Company _____

Username _____

Password _____

Notes _____

_____

_____

Name/Company _____

Username _____

Password _____

Notes _____

_____

_____

Name/Company _____

Username _____

Password _____

Notes _____

_____

_____

Name/Company _____

Username _____

Password _____

Notes _____

_____

_____

Name/Company _____

Username _____

Password _____

Notes _____

_____

_____

Name/Company _____

Username _____

Password _____

Notes _____

_____

_____

Name/Company _____

Username _____

Password _____

Notes _____

_____

_____

Name/Company _____

Username _____

Password _____

Notes _____

_____

_____

Name/Company _____

Username _____

Password _____

Notes _____

_____

_____

Name/Company _____

Username _____

Password _____

Notes _____

_____

_____

Name/Company _____

Username _____

Password _____

Notes _____

_____

_____

Name/Company _____

Username _____

Password _____

Notes _____

_____

_____

Name/Company _____

Username _____

Password _____

Notes _____

_____

_____

Name/Company _____

Username _____

Password _____

Notes _____

_____

_____

Name/Company _____

Username _____

Password _____

Notes _____

_____

_____

Name/Company _____

Username _____

Password _____

Notes _____

_____

_____

Name/Company _____

Username _____

Password _____

Notes _____

_____

_____

Name/Company _____

Username _____

Password _____

Notes _____

_____

_____

Name/Company _____

Username _____

Password _____

Notes _____

_____

_____

Name/Company _____

Username _____

Password _____

Notes _____

_____

_____

Name/Company _____

Username _____

Password _____

Notes _____

_____

_____

Name/Company _____

Username _____

Password _____

Notes _____

_____

_____

Name/Company _____

Username _____

Password _____

Notes _____

_____

_____

Name/Company _____

Username _____

Password _____

Notes _____

_____

_____

Name/Company _____

Username _____

Password _____

Notes _____

_____

_____

Name/Company _____

Username _____

Password _____

Notes _____

_____

_____

Name/Company _____

Username _____

Password _____

Notes _____

_____

_____

Name/Company _____

Username _____

Password _____

Notes _____

_____

_____

Name/Company _____

Username _____

Password _____

Notes _____

_____

_____

Name/Company _____

Username _____

Password _____

Notes _____

_____

_____

Name/Company _____

Username _____

Password _____

Notes _____

_____

_____

Name/Company _____

Username _____

Password _____

Notes _____

_____

_____

Name/Company _____

Username _____

Password _____

Notes _____

_____

_____

Name/Company _____

Username _____

Password _____

Notes _____

_____

_____

Name/Company _____

Username _____

Password _____

Notes _____

_____

_____

C
D

Name/Company _____
Username _____
Password _____
Notes _____
_____
_____

Name/Company _____
Username _____
Password _____
Notes _____
_____
_____

Name/Company _____
Username _____
Password _____
Notes _____
_____
_____

Name/Company _____
Username _____
Password _____
Notes _____
_____
_____

Name/Company _____

Username _____

Password _____

Notes _____

_____

_____

Name/Company _____

Username _____

Password _____

Notes _____

_____

_____

Name/Company _____

Username _____

Password _____

Notes _____

_____

_____

Name/Company _____

Username _____

Password _____

Notes _____

_____

_____

Name/Company _____

Username _____

Password _____

Notes _____

_____

_____

Name/Company _____

Username _____

Password _____

Notes _____

_____

_____

Name/Company _____

Username _____

Password _____

Notes _____

_____

_____

Name/Company _____

Username _____

Password _____

Notes _____

_____

_____

Name/Company _____

Username _____

Password _____

Notes _____

_____

_____

Name/Company _____

Username _____

Password _____

Notes _____

_____

_____

Name/Company _____

Username _____

Password _____

Notes _____

_____

_____

Name/Company _____

Username _____

Password _____

Notes _____

_____

_____

Name/Company _____

Username _____

Password _____

Notes _____

_____

_____

Name/Company _____

Username _____

Password _____

Notes _____

_____

_____

Name/Company _____

Username _____

Password _____

Notes _____

_____

_____

Name/Company _____

Username _____

Password _____

Notes _____

_____

_____

Name/Company _____

Username _____

Password _____

Notes _____

_____

_____

Name/Company _____

Username _____

Password _____

Notes _____

_____

_____

Name/Company _____

Username _____

Password _____

Notes _____

_____

_____

Name/Company _____

Username _____

Password _____

Notes _____

_____

_____

Name/Company _____

Username _____

Password _____

Notes _____

_____

_____

Name/Company _____

Username _____

Password _____

Notes _____

_____

_____

Name/Company _____

Username _____

Password _____

Notes _____

_____

_____

Name/Company _____

Username _____

Password _____

Notes _____

_____

_____

Name/Company _____

Username _____

Password _____

Notes _____

_____

_____

Name/Company _____

Username _____

Password _____

Notes _____

_____

_____

Name/Company _____

Username _____

Password _____

Notes _____

_____

_____

Name/Company _____

Username _____

Password _____

Notes _____

_____

_____

Name/Company _____

Username _____

Password _____

Notes _____

_____

_____

Name/Company _____

Username _____

Password _____

Notes _____

_____

_____

Name/Company _____

Username _____

Password _____

Notes _____

_____

_____

Name/Company _____

Username _____

Password _____

Notes _____

_____

_____

Name/Company _____

Username _____

Password _____

Notes _____

_____

_____

Name/Company _____

Username _____

Password _____

Notes _____

_____

_____

Name/Company _____

Username _____

Password _____

Notes _____

_____

_____

Name/Company _____

Username _____

Password _____

Notes _____

_____

_____

Name/Company _____

Username _____

Password _____

Notes _____

_____

_____

Name/Company _____

Username _____

Password _____

Notes _____

_____

_____

Name/Company _____

Username _____

Password _____

Notes _____

_____

_____

Name/Company _____

Username _____

Password _____

Notes _____

_____

_____

Name/Company _____

Username _____

Password _____

Notes _____

_____

_____

Name/Company _____

Username _____

Password _____

Notes _____

_____

_____

Name/Company _____

Username _____

Password _____

Notes _____

_____

_____

Name/Company _____

Username _____

Password _____

Notes _____

_____

_____

Name/Company _____

Username _____

Password _____

Notes _____

_____

_____

Name/Company _____

Username _____

Password _____

Notes _____

_____

_____

Name/Company _____

Username _____

Password _____

Notes _____

_____

_____

Name/Company _____

Username _____

Password _____

Notes _____

_____

_____

Name/Company _____

Username _____

Password _____

Notes _____

_____

_____

Name/Company _____

Username _____

Password _____

Notes _____

_____

_____

Name/Company _____

Username _____

Password _____

Notes _____

_____

_____

Name/Company _____

Username _____

Password _____

Notes _____

_____

_____

Name/Company _____

Username _____

Password _____

Notes _____

_____

_____

Name/Company _____

Username _____

Password _____

Notes _____

_____

_____

Name/Company _____

Username _____

Password _____

Notes _____

_____

_____

Name/Company _____

Username _____

Password _____

Notes _____

_____

_____

Name/Company _____

Username _____

Password _____

Notes _____

_____

_____

Name/Company _____

Username _____

Password _____

Notes _____

_____

_____

Name/Company _____

Username _____

Password _____

Notes _____

_____

_____

Name/Company _____

Username _____

Password _____

Notes _____

_____

_____

Name/Company _____

Username _____

Password _____

Notes _____

_____

_____

Name/Company _____

Username _____

Password _____

Notes _____

_____

_____

Name/Company _____

Username _____

Password _____

Notes _____

_____

_____

Name/Company _____

Username _____

Password _____

Notes _____

_____

_____

Name/Company _____

Username _____

Password _____

Notes _____

_____

_____

Name/Company _____

Username _____

Password _____

Notes _____

_____

_____

Name/Company _____

Username _____

Password _____

Notes _____

_____

_____

Name/Company _____

Username _____

Password _____

Notes _____

_____

_____

Name/Company _____

Username _____

Password _____

Notes _____

_____

_____

Name/Company _____

Username _____

Password _____

Notes _____

_____

_____

Name/Company _____

Username _____

Password _____

Notes _____

_____

_____

Name/Company _____

Username _____

Password _____

Notes _____

_____

_____

Name/Company _____

Username _____

Password _____

Notes _____

_____

_____

Name/Company _____

Username _____

Password _____

Notes _____

_____

_____

Name/Company _____

Username _____

Password _____

Notes _____

_____

_____

Name/Company _____

Username _____

Password _____

Notes _____

_____

_____

Name/Company _____

Username _____

Password _____

Notes _____

_____

_____

Name/Company _____

Username _____

Password _____

Notes _____

_____

_____

Name/Company _____

Username _____

Password _____

Notes _____

_____

_____

Name/Company _____

Username _____

Password _____

Notes _____

_____

_____

Name/Company _____

Username _____

Password _____

Notes _____

_____

_____

Name/Company _____

Username _____

Password _____

Notes _____

_____

_____

Name/Company _____

Username _____

Password _____

Notes _____

_____

_____

Name/Company _____

Username _____

Password _____

Notes _____

_____

_____

Name/Company _____

Username _____

Password _____

Notes _____

_____

_____

Name/Company _____

Username _____

Password _____

Notes _____

_____

_____

Name/Company _____

Username _____

Password _____

Notes _____

_____

_____

Name/Company _____

Username _____

Password _____

Notes _____

_____

_____

Name/Company _____

Username _____

Password _____

Notes _____

_____

_____

Name/Company _____

Username _____

Password _____

Notes _____

_____

_____

Name/Company _____

Username _____

Password _____

Notes _____

_____

_____

Name/Company _____

Username _____

Password _____

Notes _____

_____

_____

Name/Company _____

Username _____

Password _____

Notes _____

_____

_____

Name/Company _____

Username _____

Password _____

Notes _____

_____

_____

Name/Company _____

Username _____

Password _____

Notes _____

_____

_____

Name/Company _____

Username _____

Password _____

Notes _____

_____

_____

Name/Company _____

Username _____

Password _____

Notes _____

_____

_____

Name/Company _____

Username _____

Password _____

Notes _____

_____

_____

Name/Company _____

Username _____

Password _____

Notes _____

_____

_____

Name/Company _____

Username _____

Password _____

Notes _____

_____

_____

Name/Company _____

Username _____

Password _____

Notes _____

_____

_____

Name/Company _____

Username _____

Password _____

Notes _____

_____

_____

Name/Company _____

Username _____

Password _____

Notes _____

_____

_____

Name/Company _____

Username _____

Password _____

Notes _____

_____

_____

Name/Company _____

Username _____

Password _____

Notes _____

_____

_____

Name/Company _____

Username _____

Password _____

Notes _____

_____

_____

Name/Company _____

Username _____

Password _____

Notes _____

_____

_____

Name/Company _____

Username _____

Password _____

Notes _____

_____

_____

Name/Company _____

Username _____

Password _____

Notes _____

_____

_____

Name/Company _____

Username _____

Password _____

Notes _____

_____

_____

Name/Company _____

Username _____

Password _____

Notes _____

_____

_____

Name/Company _____

Username _____

Password _____

Notes _____

_____

_____

Name/Company _____

Username _____

Password _____

Notes _____

_____

_____

Name/Company _____

Username _____

Password _____

Notes _____

_____

_____

Name/Company _____

Username _____

Password _____

Notes _____

_____

_____

Name/Company _____

Username _____

Password _____

Notes _____

_____

_____

Name/Company _____

Username _____

Password _____

Notes _____

_____

_____

Name/Company _____

Username _____

Password _____

Notes _____

_____

_____

Name/Company _____

Username _____

Password _____

Notes _____

_____

_____

Name/Company _____

Username _____

Password _____

Notes _____

_____

_____

Name/Company _____

Username _____

Password _____

Notes _____

_____

_____

Name/Company _____

Username _____

Password _____

Notes _____

_____

_____

Name/Company _____

Username _____

Password _____

Notes _____

_____

_____

Name/Company _____

Username _____

Password _____

Notes _____

_____

_____

Name/Company _____

Username _____

Password _____

Notes _____

_____

_____

Name/Company _____

Username _____

Password _____

Notes _____

_____

_____

Name/Company _____

Username _____

Password _____

Notes _____

_____

_____

Name/Company _____

Username _____

Password _____

Notes _____

_____

_____

Name/Company _____

Username _____

Password _____

Notes _____

_____

_____

Name/Company _____

Username _____

Password _____

Notes _____

_____

_____

Name/Company _____

Username _____

Password _____

Notes _____

_____

_____

Name/Company _____

Username _____

Password _____

Notes _____

_____

_____

Name/Company _____

Username _____

Password _____

Notes _____

_____

_____

Name/Company _____

Username _____

Password _____

Notes _____

_____

_____

Name/Company _____

Username _____

Password _____

Notes _____

_____

_____

Name/Company _____

Username _____

Password _____

Notes _____

_____

_____

Name/Company _____

Username _____

Password _____

Notes _____

_____

_____

Name/Company _____

Username _____

Password _____

Notes _____

_____

_____

Name/Company _____

Username _____

Password _____

Notes _____

_____

_____

Name/Company _____

Username _____

Password _____

Notes _____

_____

_____

Name/Company _____

Username _____

Password _____

Notes _____

_____

_____

Name/Company _____

Username _____

Password _____

Notes _____

_____

_____

Name/Company _____

Username _____

Password _____

Notes _____

_____

_____

Name/Company _____

Username _____

Password _____

Notes _____

_____

_____

Name/Company _____

Username _____

Password _____

Notes _____

_____

_____

Name/Company _____

Username _____

Password _____

Notes _____

_____

_____

Name/Company _____

Username _____

Password _____

Notes _____

_____

_____

Name/Company _____

Username _____

Password _____

Notes _____

_____

_____

Name/Company _____

Username _____

Password _____

Notes _____

_____

_____

Name/Company _____

Username _____

Password _____

Notes _____

_____

_____

Name/Company _____

Username _____

Password _____

Notes _____

_____

_____

Name/Company _____

Username _____

Password _____

Notes _____

_____

_____

Name/Company _____

Username _____

Password _____

Notes _____

_____

_____

Name/Company _____

Username _____

Password _____

Notes _____

_____

_____

Name/Company _____

Username _____

Password _____

Notes _____

_____

_____

Name/Company _____

Username _____

Password _____

Notes _____

_____

_____

Name/Company _____

Username _____

Password _____

Notes _____

_____

_____

Name/Company _____

Username _____

Password _____

Notes _____

_____

_____

Name/Company _____

Username _____

Password _____

Notes _____

_____

_____

Name/Company _____

Username _____

Password _____

Notes _____

_____

_____

Name/Company _____

Username _____

Password _____

Notes _____

_____

_____

Name/Company _____

Username _____

Password _____

Notes _____

_____

_____

Name/Company _____

Username _____

Password _____

Notes _____

_____

_____

Name/Company _____

Username _____

Password _____

Notes _____

_____

_____

Name/Company _____

Username _____

Password _____

Notes _____

_____

_____

Name/Company _____

Username _____

Password _____

Notes _____

_____

_____

M
N

Name/Company _____

Username _____

Password _____

Notes _____

_____

_____

Name/Company _____

Username _____

Password _____

Notes _____

_____

_____

Name/Company _____

Username _____

Password _____

Notes _____

_____

_____

Name/Company _____

Username _____

Password _____

Notes _____

_____

_____

Name/Company _____

Username _____

Password _____

Notes _____

_____

_____

Name/Company _____

Username _____

Password _____

Notes _____

_____

_____

Name/Company _____

Username _____

Password _____

Notes _____

_____

_____

Name/Company _____

Username _____

Password _____

Notes _____

_____

_____

Name/Company _____

Username _____

Password _____

Notes _____

_____

_____

Name/Company _____

Username _____

Password _____

Notes _____

_____

_____

Name/Company _____

Username _____

Password _____

Notes _____

_____

_____

Name/Company _____

Username _____

Password _____

Notes _____

_____

_____

O
P

Name/Company _____

Username _____

Password _____

Notes _____

_____

_____

Name/Company _____

Username _____

Password _____

Notes _____

_____

_____

Name/Company _____

Username _____

Password _____

Notes _____

_____

_____

Name/Company _____

Username _____

Password _____

Notes _____

_____

_____

Name/Company _____

Username _____

Password _____

Notes _____

_____

_____

Name/Company _____

Username _____

Password _____

Notes _____

_____

_____

Name/Company _____

Username _____

Password _____

Notes _____

_____

_____

Name/Company _____

Username _____

Password _____

Notes _____

_____

_____

Name/Company _____

Username _____

Password _____

Notes _____

_____

_____

Name/Company _____

Username _____

Password _____

Notes _____

_____

_____

Name/Company _____

Username _____

Password _____

Notes _____

_____

_____

Name/Company _____

Username _____

Password _____

Notes _____

_____

_____

Name/Company _____

Username _____

Password _____

Notes _____

_____

_____

O
P

Name/Company _____

Username _____

Password _____

Notes _____

_____

_____

Name/Company _____

Username _____

Password _____

Notes _____

_____

_____

Name/Company _____

Username _____

Password _____

Notes _____

_____

_____

Name/Company _____

Username _____

Password _____

Notes _____

_____

_____

Name/Company _____

Username _____

Password _____

Notes _____

_____

_____

Name/Company _____

Username _____

Password _____

Notes _____

_____

_____

Name/Company _____

Username _____

Password _____

Notes _____

_____

_____

Name/Company _____

Username _____

Password _____

Notes _____

_____

_____

O
P

Name/Company _____

Username _____

Password _____

Notes _____

_____

_____

Name/Company _____

Username _____

Password _____

Notes _____

_____

_____

Name/Company _____

Username _____

Password _____

Notes _____

_____

_____

Name/Company _____

Username _____

Password _____

Notes _____

_____

_____

Name/Company _____

Username _____

Password _____

Notes _____

_____

_____

Name/Company _____

Username _____

Password _____

Notes _____

_____

_____

Name/Company _____

Username _____

Password _____

Notes _____

_____

_____

Name/Company _____

Username _____

Password _____

Notes _____

_____

_____

Name/Company _____

Username _____

Password _____

Notes _____

_____

_____

Name/Company _____

Username _____

Password _____

Notes _____

_____

_____

Name/Company _____

Username _____

Password _____

Notes _____

_____

_____

Name/Company _____

Username _____

Password _____

Notes _____

_____

_____

Name/Company _____

Username _____

Password _____

Notes _____

_____

_____

Name/Company _____

Username _____

Password _____

Notes _____

_____

_____

Name/Company _____

Username _____

Password _____

Notes _____

_____

_____

Name/Company _____

Username _____

Password _____

Notes _____

_____

_____

Name/Company _____

Username _____

Password _____

Notes _____

_____

_____

Name/Company _____

Username _____

Password _____

Notes _____

_____

_____

Name/Company _____

Username _____

Password _____

Notes _____

_____

_____

Name/Company _____

Username _____

Password _____

Notes _____

_____

_____

Name/Company _____

Username _____

Password _____

Notes _____

_____

_____

Name/Company _____

Username _____

Password _____

Notes _____

_____

_____

Name/Company _____

Username _____

Password _____

Notes _____

_____

_____

Name/Company _____

Username _____

Password _____

Notes _____

_____

_____

Name/Company _____

Username _____

Password _____

Notes _____

_____

_____

Name/Company _____

Username _____

Password _____

Notes _____

_____

_____

Name/Company _____

Username _____

Password _____

Notes _____

_____

_____

Name/Company _____

Username _____

Password _____

Notes _____

_____

_____

Name/Company _____

Username _____

Password _____

Notes _____

_____

_____

Name/Company _____

Username _____

Password _____

Notes _____

_____

_____

Name/Company _____

Username _____

Password _____

Notes _____

_____

_____

Name/Company _____

Username _____

Password _____

Notes _____

_____

_____

Name/Company _____

Username _____

Password _____

Notes _____

_____

_____

Name/Company _____

Username _____

Password _____

Notes _____

_____

_____

Name/Company _____

Username _____

Password _____

Notes _____

_____

_____

Name/Company _____

Username _____

Password _____

Notes _____

_____

_____

Name/Company _____

Username _____

Password _____

Notes _____

_____

_____

Name/Company _____

Username _____

Password _____

Notes _____

_____

_____

Name/Company _____

Username _____

Password _____

Notes _____

_____

_____

Name/Company _____

Username _____

Password _____

Notes _____

_____

_____

Name/Company _____

Username _____

Password _____

Notes _____

_____

_____

Name/Company _____

Username _____

Password _____

Notes _____

_____

_____

Name/Company _____

Username _____

Password _____

Notes _____

_____

_____

Name/Company _____

Username _____

Password _____

Notes _____

_____

_____

S
T

Name/Company _____

Username _____

Password _____

Notes _____

_____

_____

Name/Company _____

Username _____

Password _____

Notes _____

_____

_____

Name/Company _____

Username _____

Password _____

Notes _____

_____

_____

Name/Company _____

Username _____

Password _____

Notes _____

_____

_____

Name/Company _____

Username _____

Password _____

Notes _____

_____

_____

Name/Company _____

Username _____

Password _____

Notes _____

_____

_____

Name/Company _____

Username _____

Password _____

Notes _____

_____

_____

Name/Company _____

Username _____

Password _____

Notes _____

_____

_____

Name/Company _____

Username _____

Password _____

Notes _____

_____

_____

Name/Company _____

Username _____

Password _____

Notes _____

_____

_____

Name/Company _____

Username _____

Password _____

Notes _____

_____

_____

Name/Company _____

Username _____

Password _____

Notes _____

_____

_____

Name/Company _____

Username _____

Password _____

Notes _____

_____

_____

Name/Company _____

Username _____

Password _____

Notes _____

_____

_____

Name/Company _____

Username _____

Password _____

Notes _____

_____

_____

Name/Company _____

Username _____

Password _____

Notes _____

_____

_____

S
T

Name/Company _____

Username _____

Password _____

Notes _____

_____

_____

Name/Company _____

Username _____

Password _____

Notes _____

_____

_____

Name/Company _____

Username _____

Password _____

Notes _____

_____

_____

Name/Company _____

Username _____

Password _____

Notes _____

_____

_____

Name/Company _____

Username _____

Password _____

Notes _____

_____

_____

Name/Company _____

Username _____

Password _____

Notes _____

_____

_____

Name/Company _____

Username _____

Password _____

Notes _____

_____

_____

Name/Company _____

Username _____

Password _____

Notes _____

_____

_____

Name/Company _____

Username _____

Password _____

Notes _____

_____

_____

Name/Company _____

Username _____

Password _____

Notes _____

_____

_____

Name/Company _____

Username _____

Password _____

Notes _____

_____

_____

Name/Company _____

Username _____

Password _____

Notes _____

_____

_____

Name/Company _____

Username _____

Password _____

Notes _____

_____

_____

U
V

Name/Company _____

Username _____

Password _____

Notes _____

_____

_____

Name/Company _____

Username _____

Password _____

Notes _____

_____

_____

Name/Company _____

Username _____

Password _____

Notes _____

_____

_____

Name/Company _____

Username _____

Password _____

Notes _____

_____

_____

Name/Company _____

Username _____

Password _____

Notes _____

_____

_____

Name/Company _____

Username _____

Password _____

Notes _____

_____

_____

Name/Company _____

Username _____

Password _____

Notes _____

_____

_____

Name/Company _____

Username _____

Password _____

Notes _____

_____

_____

U
V

Name/Company _____

Username _____

Password _____

Notes _____

_____

_____

Name/Company _____

Username _____

Password _____

Notes _____

_____

_____

Name/Company _____

Username _____

Password _____

Notes _____

_____

_____

Name/Company _____

Username _____

Password _____

Notes _____

_____

_____

U
V

Name/Company _____

Username _____

Password _____

Notes _____

_____

_____

Name/Company _____

Username _____

Password _____

Notes _____

_____

_____

Name/Company _____

Username _____

Password _____

Notes _____

_____

_____

Name/Company _____

Username _____

Password _____

Notes _____

_____

_____

Name/Company _____

Username _____

Password _____

Notes _____

_____

_____

Name/Company _____

Username _____

Password _____

Notes _____

_____

_____

Name/Company _____

Username _____

Password _____

Notes _____

_____

_____

Name/Company _____

Username _____

Password _____

Notes _____

_____

_____

Name/Company _____

Username _____

Password _____

Notes _____

_____

_____

Name/Company _____

Username _____

Password _____

Notes _____

_____

_____

Name/Company _____

Username _____

Password _____

Notes _____

_____

_____

Name/Company _____

Username _____

Password _____

Notes _____

_____

_____

Name/Company _____

Username _____

Password _____

Notes _____

_____

_____

Name/Company _____

Username _____

Password _____

Notes _____

_____

_____

Name/Company _____

Username _____

Password _____

Notes _____

_____

_____

Name/Company _____

Username _____

Password _____

Notes _____

_____

_____

U
V

Name/Company _____

Username _____

Password _____

Notes _____

_____

_____

Name/Company _____

Username _____

Password _____

Notes _____

_____

_____

Name/Company _____

Username _____

Password _____

Notes _____

_____

_____

Name/Company _____

Username _____

Password _____

Notes _____

W
X

_____

_____

Name/Company _____

Username _____

Password _____

Notes _____

_____

_____

Name/Company _____

Username _____

Password _____

Notes _____

_____

_____

Name/Company _____

Username _____

Password _____

Notes _____

_____

_____

Name/Company _____

Username _____

Password _____

Notes _____

_____

_____

W
X

Name/Company _____

Username _____

Password _____

Notes _____

_____

_____

Name/Company _____

Username _____

Password _____

Notes _____

_____

_____

Name/Company _____

Username _____

Password _____

Notes _____

_____

_____

Name/Company _____

Username _____

Password _____

Notes _____

_____

_____

Name/Company _____

Username _____

Password _____

Notes _____

_____

_____

Name/Company _____

Username _____

Password _____

Notes _____

_____

_____

Name/Company _____

Username _____

Password _____

Notes _____

_____

_____

Name/Company _____

Username _____

Password _____

Notes _____

_____

_____

Name/Company _____

Username _____

Password _____

Notes _____

_____

_____

Name/Company _____

Username _____

Password _____

Notes _____

_____

_____

Name/Company _____

Username _____

Password _____

Notes _____

_____

_____

Name/Company _____

Username _____

Password _____

Notes _____

_____

W
X

_____

Name/Company _____

Username _____

Password _____

Notes _____

_____

_____

Name/Company _____

Username _____

Password _____

Notes _____

_____

_____

Name/Company _____

Username _____

Password _____

Notes _____

_____

_____

Name/Company _____

Username _____

Password _____

Notes _____

_____

_____

W
X

Name/Company _____

Username _____

Password _____

Notes _____

_____

_____

Name/Company _____

Username _____

Password _____

Notes _____

_____

_____

Name/Company _____

Username _____

Password _____

Notes _____

_____

_____

Name/Company _____

Username _____

Password _____

Notes _____

W
X

_____

_____

Name/Company _____

Username _____

Password _____

Notes _____

_____

_____

Name/Company _____

Username _____

Password _____

Notes _____

_____

_____

Name/Company _____

Username _____

Password _____

Notes _____

_____

_____

Name/Company _____

Username _____

Password _____

Notes _____

_____

_____

W
X

Name/Company _____

Username _____

Password _____

Notes _____

_____

_____

Name/Company _____

Username _____

Password _____

Notes _____

_____

_____

Name/Company _____

Username _____

Password _____

Notes _____

_____

_____

Name/Company _____

Username _____

Password _____

Notes _____

_____

_____

Name/Company _____

Username _____

Password _____

Notes _____

_____

_____

Name/Company _____

Username _____

Password _____

Notes _____

_____

_____

Name/Company _____

Username _____

Password _____

Notes _____

_____

_____

Name/Company _____

Username _____

Password _____

Notes _____

_____

_____

Y
Z

Name/Company _____

Username _____

Password _____

Notes _____

_____

_____

Name/Company _____

Username _____

Password _____

Notes _____

_____

_____

Name/Company _____

Username _____

Password _____

Notes _____

_____

_____

Name/Company _____

Username _____

Password _____

Notes _____

_____

_____

Name/Company _____

Username _____

Password _____

Notes _____

_____

_____

Name/Company _____

Username _____

Password _____

Notes _____

_____

_____

Name/Company _____

Username _____

Password _____

Notes _____

_____

_____

Name/Company _____

Username _____

Password _____

Notes _____

_____

_____

Y
Z

Name/Company _____

Username _____

Password _____

Notes _____

_____

_____

Name/Company _____

Username _____

Password _____

Notes _____

_____

_____

Name/Company _____

Username _____

Password _____

Notes _____

_____

_____

Name/Company _____

Username _____

Password _____

Notes _____

_____

_____

Y
Z

Router/Wireless Network 1

Factory-default Admin IP Address _____

Factory-default Username _____

Factory-default Password _____

User-defined Admin IP Address _____

User-defined Username _____

User-defined Password _____

Router/Wireless Network 2

Factory-default Admin IP Address _____

Factory-default Username _____

Factory-default Password _____

User-defined Admin IP Address _____

User-defined Username _____

User-defined Password _____

Clematis, Mary Emily Eaton, 1916

Dicentra, Mary Vaux Walcott, 1925

NOTES